Is America Used Up?

Is America Used Up?

Judith Mara Gutman

Grossman Publishers *New York* *1973*

Copyright © 1973 by Judith Mara Gutman
All rights reserved
First published in 1973 by Grossman Publishers
625 Madison Avenue, New York, N.Y. 10022
Published simultaneously in Canada by
Fitzhenry and Whiteside, Ltd.
SBN 670-40180-3
Library of Congress Catalogue Card Number: 72-77699
Printed in U.S.A.

This book was set on the linotype in Century Expanded
The display type is Century Expanded italic
The composition is by Maryland Linotype Composition Co.
The printing and binding is by Halliday Lithographers
Designed by Jacqueline Schuman

We know the golden granulated grail of give and grab is used up. Not by any plan, but just worked itself out of existence. Simply doesn't exist anymore. Where do we turn? This book is dedicated to those who shape new forms of life. Meager or grotesque: doesn't matter. As long as they have the sharp raw edges of a passion.

Contents

Is America Used Up?

Is America used up? Is the strength and expression of America —the idea that we can produce and enlarge our central notions of freedom, then enlarge them still further in spite of our ills— is that idea used up? Is the belief that we could expand the freedom and expression which we always rather automatically assumed came with life in America—is that worn out? It's an uneasy thought. We don't like its edge. We want to dismiss it.

Because we *are* getting used up. We move more hesitantly, try to run risk out of our lives, and become more wary about reaching far-off ends. We've lost the surety and conviction that we formerly gained from living on an edge that we could never predictably know was going to provide a firm footing. We've lost the belief in what we could create, not in what we did create, but the belief in our ability to establish a new order of life should we want to.

And indeed we don't take chances in creating anew. Where we used to plunge into new areas with a certain delight for the unpredictable goals we would reach, now we want sure results and try to calculate the consequences an act will bring. Where we moved with a certain flair for the new life we might turn up, now we hem in our vision and don't think of new life however exciting it may promise to be. I'm not suggesting there's a change in the substantive character of what we want. We still want power, for instance—always have and probably always will, both as people and as a nation. But I am suggesting there's a change in the kind of power we wanted then and what we want now, a change in the kind of reach we used earlier and what we use now. Today we want to close up the gaps in our lives. Where we formerly felt comfortable in unbalancing our lives and even felt calm and easy about letting unknown ends tempt us in our desire to gain, now we measure our steps and want to be sure of the responses each move will bring. The old reaches seem risky. They throw us off-balance. We prefer settling our lives down and letting a smooth easy flow mediate what is sharp and jarring in our lives.

So we never experience the fulfillment a riskier search brought. Wanting an ordered lineup of life, we tend to think of our society as one of institutions rather than as one of people. Don't we define our workday by the wage-earning or salaried jobs the society offers? Don't we think of our government as a structure rather than as a reflected body of desires? And don't we think of our communities in terms of the schools, organizations, and churches it offers rather than with either the footloose or established expressions running through those communities? Even as critics we let our society's structure set the terms for our thoughts. Haven't we been told for the past twenty-five years that one or another of our institutional structures, whether it be government, technology, or the war machine, is dominating our lives? And don't we then argue which institution most clearly disturbs us, assuming, of course, that that critical vision is complete and that one of those institutions is the most crucial determinant of our lives?

Few of us focus on the losses of expression an individual experiences, and when we do, see those losses as part of the institutional patterns that blanket our lives. We even think with an institutionalized conception of individualism, ready to cheer or berate it, but accepting its pegs as the ones upon which we hang all behavioral patterns and codes. It's as if an individual must belong to the institutions that surround him for us to recognize and understand his existence, as if those institutions provide a backbone for all lives. Even the young tend to rely on such institutional patterns. Many who want to strike out on their own assume the society's institutions into their life styles as they adopt the most orderly housekeeping arrangements with the most standard divisions of labor between them. Rather than run with the delight, fear, and satisfactions that come from venturing, we lean back on our institutions. As if they would strengthen our lives.

Earlier we never did. Americans used to think they could build their systems of life, that they didn't need to walk into an already structured setup and take their place at desk or

machine. More, they used to believe that in the very process of working and building those systems they would become freer and fuller. In the early part of the nineteenth century, for instance, the mechanic still thought of himself as an artist and used his inventive capacity to refine and create tools and processes. The interior of New York's Crystal Palace threaded new delicate reaches into its mechanical artistic sweep.

Later in the century Americans adapted that mechanical thrust to the power they saw growing out of the factory. Not that they had to work in a factory. They rather expected they only had to be a part of the new bubbling society with all it could produce, that being a part of it would make them a part of its fruition. They transformed the satisfaction they realized from working as a mechanic to working in a factory and then to the society at large. By the twentieth century many who never recognized a lathe or plow nor were ever in a factory still expected fruition through work. It was as if the image of that effusive productive life assured all who worked at whatever trade they chose that they would have the power to create their society. Not just live in it but create it.

That's no longer true. Automobile workers in Detroit rail against their union, scoff at their employers, some even jam up the processes of production. Construction workers throw and drop rivets from the high-set beams upon which they work. White-collar workers come to work later and slough off the jobs they used to do with pride. Even the self-employed cabinetmaker who more independently chooses his work and would seem to be freeing himself from restraints feels caught by an economy that often determines just what he can and cannot make. Americans no longer bank on expecting to find personal satisfaction through their work.

We've even begun to drop out of work while staying fixed to the job. Cars come off the assembly line with slashed seats and malfunctioning brakes. Doors don't close on refrigerators. Shoes come apart at the seams. Washing machines break down in their first year. And television repairmen don't repair the sets they set out to fix. We've become less attached to the things and people with whom we work.

Many of us turn to our communities as if we might find some comfort in the order they bring. Not that we melt into a community's patterns; indeed many of us take our place at school-board meetings, form block associations, and actually become part of the decision-making body for a community. Adopting the word "neighborhood," we try to imagine some of the exhilarations and fulfillments we expect from our lives through that community. But we soon realize that even though the decisions we make are effective and in keeping with the word "neighborhood," they don't create a new order of life. We begin to realize that however much we live with our communities and their institutions, we don't shape the character and style of life we lead in them. The "neighborhood" we imagined turns out to be an image of a life that others led there seventy years ago and not one we can build today. It's as if the process of building a community belonged to another day and age and another way of life, as if the power that a local concentric turning of life produces is insufficient.

We let things be. If we can't change anything, what's the use? Anyway, isn't our government too big, unwieldy, and corrupt? We can elect a better man, even vote for someone who wants to overhaul much of our structure. But even after we do that we expect that he will only have trimmed off the excess. We know we can't fight city hall; and whoever heard of a petition to clean up the streets or build better schools changing the character of our lives? We might get cleaner streets or better schools, but we don't feel the satisfaction we expected from either the petition or the reform.

We go on to assume that even when the chips are down we can't do anything to our form of government, that our government can't open new areas of satisfaction, that essentially the process of governing has reached a saturation point. It can't yield any further results and that's the way it's going to be. Forget it, we tell ourselves, that as long as we have our guarantee of freedom that's pretty much okay. Anyway, it's the best we can do and all we can expect. We settle for the barest, most minimal conception of government and coast along on that.

In the same way, we've come to agree that our cities have reached a dead end, that they can become prettied up but not generate any new life. We don't think of hidden greatness coming out of our cities but rather look at the eruption of burglaries and murders and decide we should get rid of the ugliness and mess and at least make cities safe so people can walk in the streets and not get robbed, raped, or murdered. To think of a city offering new life is out of line: it can't even take care of its old. With the same frame of mind, we think cities are fun and when we visit buy clothes, go to museums, even go to a concert or two and look at the new buildings that smooth out our lives. We think of a city offering divertissement and fringes to a life we lead elsewhere but never think of a city generating the substance of a life we lead daily.

We've even given up the belief that liberty and justice can bloom, that each has an internal unexpressed life which is still to open up. We rather think of liberty and justice as wholly formed units, as standards against which we measure our lives and decide if we are faring well or poorly but never if they have grown. That's very different from the conception of liberty that James Madison used in 1787 in *The Federalist* when he warned against dousing the fires that may rage around liberty for fear they would strike down *its* life. In the same way it is far different from the trembling new life that Eugene Victor Debs expected from a Socialist State. And very different from the assumptions that Justice Oliver Wendell Holmes used in widening earlier definitions of liberty as he annotated Kent's *Commentaries* in the 1870s. Whether Madisonian, Socialist, or bordering on the upper-class caste of nineteenth-century Brahmins, one always assumed that liberty and justice each had a yet to be expressed life, that they would germinate futures one could not predictably describe in the present. Rather than thinking of them only as bases or bulwarks from which American life might grow, one thought of them as unfinished, yet to be determined concepts. At the same time they opened expressions for others, they widened and deepened their own dimensions.

It's not that different groups don't want justice and liberty today, or even that Brahmins, Socialists, or early republicans always expanded the meaning of justice and liberty. They often didn't. But they assumed they would . . . and today when radicals say we should have greater justice and conservatives defend its principles they're both using a conception whose end limits are definable and complete. Don't we talk of "giving" justice, as if we could mete it out, as if it was a known entity and all we had to do was properly apportion it? And don't we often run it into our conceptions of decency, letting the two become a mixture that we are ready to say represents the best in American life—you know, those good common decent values that have always made America great? In effect, of course, we reduce justice when we speak of it as decency because as admirable a fact of American life as decency is, it is something less than the justice and liberty that were going to ring through the land and allow one to build the still more human expressions one expected he would.

In anger we cry out against the telephone companies, rail against the train systems, and damn the plane companies. Some of us walk defiantly through parks at night as if to prove we at least still have that decency, that one is not automatically going to be molested. We find a way to defend the most minimal conditions and then try to tell ourselves that life is okay, that it isn't that bad. But in unleashing our anger we find symbols of decay and in pointing at those symbols we move further from the possibility of creating the very power we need. We stab out at some clear obvious ill that becomes the bête noir for all that has gone wrong in American life and either attack or define the bête noir—or find another—but get sucked into thinking with it rather than with the loss of life with which we all live. We find a way that allows our used up condition to continue instead of building the power we need to make our lives freer and fuller, as if by venting our feelings and alleviating our pain we could re-establish some of the greatness of human expression we once associated with America.

But of course the greatness grew out of another frame of mind. It grew out of an adventurous desire to search and expand. Those who moved across or into the country in the eighteenth and nineteenth centuries expected to build new ways. Reformers battling against exploitation and the denial of life to women, children, and workers in the late nineteenth and early twentieth centuries expected to build totally new communities and change the course of American life. Even Americans who were thrown by the depression of the 1930s expected to create, build, and replenish the life they saw wasting around them. The greatness of American life always grew out of a belief that one could and would build. No one really thought that America could ever be used up.

Today we're not so sure about that. We've become afraid of confronting old age. It's not that we run from it but rather that we wish we wouldn't have to face it. So we put our mothers and fathers in nursing homes where we meet and talk with them but don't live with either the problems of growing old or the fruition it brings. It's as if by not meeting it head-on but dealing with it a little bit and realizing a minimal appreciation of it we do something about it. With the same middling vacillation, we deal with old buildings, at one minute delighted with the subsumed glory they exude as we fix up their exteriors and show how great they once were; at the next isolating one and turning it into a monument; and at still another tearing down every blasted old building we see to look at those spanking new structures that stand in the gleaming sun, delighted as we spin up a roadway to enter glass doors surrounded by spraying white fountains that suggest the promise of new life

we want but doubt we will have.

We tell ourselves that we should be content to live in America, that even though it has problems it is still pretty much the best place around, that we can live in all those clean marvelous new structures, that everybody has more now than they ever did, that we need to fix up some of the laws, that after all it isn't that bad—we do have something. We accept the minimum and assume that that's all right, that we'll get along, that we'll just build little molehills rather than mountains. Don't we need to start small, anyway? We've come to back up the most minimal conditions of human expression and assume that maybe we don't have a right to any more. Where we used to assume that we would build the maximum, now we settle into that depleted hollow that generates no life or thought. We focus on the reductions with which we live to prove we still have some of the greatness.

Some of us, of course, locate some of the real problems that have grown around us, fingering the coal companies, for instance, for the easy cheap ways they permanently deplete an area as they strip-mine coal, destroy the mines' inner seams, and release poisonous gases to kill off surrounding vegetation. More than venting our outrage we locate a real problem and pour our forces into stopping it. We seem to be locating what has gone wrong.

But why do we assume that the solution to our problems is to stop life when we used to think it was to build? Why do we think we are living a good life when we keep things at bay when we used to think that living the good life meant creating? Why do we assume that all we can do is hold life in balance when we used to think we could propel it into new balances? Why do we acquiesce to circles we formerly set into motion? Why do we think that we must live in this suspended middle, that this holding action will create the good life when the essence of American life always grew out of the unpredictable, sometimes wild with violence, but always committed belief in the enlarged sense of life a person would build? Why have we become so desperate about doing something, just anything, as if that was the epitome of what we might create?

Because we've come to accept the used up nature of our lives. Natural resources, for instance, have been eroding for a long time. The buffalo was extinct by the end of the nineteenth century and the oyster beds that the Dutch saw in the waters around Manhattan in 1620 were dried up by the time of the American Revolution. That was two hundred years ago. I'm not suggesting that we should or shouldn't have done something about them, but rather looking at the fact that we didn't, that we never really thought they were used up even though we knew they were, that we never thought that something could be used up.

It's only in the last decades that we know with certainty. Not that we fooled ourselves earlier but rather that we always saw alternatives, that we always thought that as bad, low, or scraping-bottom as our lives were becoming, we could do something about them. We still assumed we had that power, that we didn't need to think of either oysters or ourselves being used up. But in the last decades we've closed out those possibilities. We fasten onto the resources that are wearing thin and demonstrate against their loss, as if by turning those losses into a rallying cry we would be doing something about the real hollows in our lives.

Meanwhile we go about our business on that less expectant plane and assume it's normal, letting the notion of a used up life become an implicit part of the way we think. Schoolchildren, for instance, think the word atomic refers only to the bomb and the destruction it brings, not to the resources of atomic energy from which it grew. They have no notion of the bomb being a by-product of the age's scientific potential nor do they think of science in terms of unleashed energies. To them, as indeed to much of the adult population, science is a completed predictable accounting of theoretical notions, not a tenuous search for new expression. In the same way, the man entering his forties and fifties doesn't think of unused skills and talents he may have but rather of what he has already done, often telling himself that he's going to make them work even more successfully, in effect unwinding and finishing out known predictable accounts of himself. Even when he does turn to a new job he often chooses one that lives under the umbrella of the first, rarely choosing to live with new facts and ideas. As if he had nothing else to come to life. No untapped resources.

With politics and political power we think no differently. The move to give federal and state aid to cities is discussed around the question of shifting monies that are already conceived, even raising the debt, but never discussed around the question of how to create new monies or how a city could expand into a different unit of life. Similarly, the process of redistricting an electoral unit depends on the notion that power must be held in balance, that it must never be allowed to expand. When new boundary lines for a district are drawn, the other party, whichever it is, always expects to gain, but it conceives of its gains by rebalancing what already exists—by taking some of the power it can measure—not by taking the chance of building power out of fermenting new life.

Meanwhile conservatives tell everyone to go back to some earlier day and sit under the old oak tree and not even try to rebalance money or power. Just use those good decent leftover values and whatever else sifts down from the past, especially, they warn us, to be prudent and sure we don't use too much freedom. We might use it up, they tell us.

If we heard that at any point in our lives up to the 1890s regardless of which part of the political spectrum we favored or how little violence we tended to use, we would consider that a treasonous attack on the very assumptions of American life. One could only use freedom with abandon. One could only let freedom pour out its unpredictable quantities and spread its possible fire. Freedom meant the potential of expression it carried, the new ideas it germinated. To be free one couldn't calculate the nature of expression. One had to risk, search, and go off the deep end. One couldn't provide only so much and no more freedom than a prescribed amount. One had to let ideas infect each other, one either prodding or hanging onto another but challenging it and its whole blasted stream of thought. Freedom grew out of a cross-fertilization. Didn't the ferment and conflict of the 1780s produce the Constitution? Didn't the diverse developments of the 1850s come out of the mix of people and hopes that had never before shared the same soil? And didn't the chaotic and bloody conflicts of the Victorian and Industrial worlds produce new freedoms before those freedoms were swallowed into giant new systems of power? To be free one had to force open the flow of life, not seal up its leaks and hold back its flow.

But one takes that kind of chance because he feels sure that he can shape his life. And today we don't. We don't feel we have that power. More, no sooner do we hear someone challenging our use of freedom and telling us we are squandering its use than we retreat into some cubbyhole, uncomfortable perhaps, but protected from harsh risky winds, sure that no good will come out of all that risk anyway. So what if we aren't any freer? Don't we have the best and most freedom? Anyway, maybe they are sort of right. Perhaps we are a bit too brash with the amount of freedom we allow. After all, we do have to be careful about the man who calls fire in a theater. There have to be some sort of limits. We can't let the desire for expression run rampant. Maybe we don't need all that freedom. Anyway, if we don't use so much of it maybe the fuss over its use will just go away. Hiding and retreating further, we yield to the demands to squelch even the minimum to which we've already been reduced. We take away freedom's guts, then, in our diminished state, say we really couldn't be much freer anyway.

So we never get near thinking of the magnificence we could build, never get near thinking about questions of human greatness and the maximum state of life such greatness could bring about. We never get near thinking, for instance, of how an individual's untapped resources can expand the character and nature of our lives, or of how an individual's unleashed energy can become a social unit of power. Much more involved with immediate problems, we try to bargain for the better of two minimal conditions, like trying to decide if it's better to live in a boring suburb or gangster-ridden city. As if notions of greatness were foreign, we think that the idea of using an individual's unused power, for instance, to reshape our government is out of touch—just out of the realm of possibility. In the same way we also think that the idea of making our unexpressed scientific energies create new human dimensions is way out of line—just implausible. And indeed these thoughts are out of range. They're all out of the range of our used up state of mind. Closing ourselves into used up cycles, we never get near thinking of maximum life.

Thinking within the used up framework, we come to expect that everything will continue out of the patterns of the past, that all we have to do is accept or reject an outline of life that already exists. In effect, of course, we yield our unexpressed power whether we accept or reject. For whichever we choose, we exist at the beck and call of some other force and turn ourselves into rote human beings. Giving up the power we might build to turn the course and direction of cities, government, or the organization of the workday, we give up our individual expression, then think that it is simply not within the realm of human power to create and control life. We say it can't exist. Just rule it out.

But by giving up the conception of controlling one's life, by canceling that notion out of our much cherished decent normal swell, we reduce the booming blossoming power we always expected to build. We take away its guts. We tell ourselves that we can't chart our course, that there is nothing to choose from, that freedom has none of the magic or power we once expected it did; can't even find it on the horizon. Wiping out possibilities, we deaden our senses and still our minds. Kill ourselves off. Like genocide.

So where do we turn? Can we? Do we have any course? Can we produce new energy? Construct new principles and reaches?

We can try. Start in two ways. For one we can try to locate where and how the used up process started, where and how we started to let our expression diverge from the freedom that first spawned it. We can see what our expression looked like when we let it run rampant and what our freedom looked like when *it* was flowering. We can also see how our various forms of expression spun off their own by-products. Then see how we let some of our illusions flower so that we might extend our expression—see that happen even though we were already hemming in our freedom. The next two sections of this book do that. They show our many forms of expression, but they don't show too much of our freedom because by the end of the nineteenth century, when much of this book begins to grow, much of that freedom was already becoming stagnant. Existing but hanging on. With life, but unregenerative. They'll show how we've hung onto both illusionary and real forms of expression that did take root.

Secondly, we can look further into our society today, see its meanderings, underpinnings, and movements and examine the expression that has no tie to the dominant older framework that once bore it. In the fourth section we will see how our used up clamp holds us in place and keeps us from experimenting, finally see unbalancing, untied, counterpointed forms of expression forcing our vision wider, opening our minds to new conceptions of freedom. That notion has lain dormant for a century.

We should find ourselves on a venturesome new ledge, secured only to the possible new life we will be creating.

When Possibilities Were Realities

Americans used to think they could expand the contentment that ran through their lives, that they could make the forms of their lives, like their class, work, or the place of nature, carry their expression. More than forcing their structures into a rote corner of their lives, then dreaming of some hazy better day with another, they expected to make their expression flow through the structures they built. They expected to fuse the two, to shape the specific forms of their better life; and to do so by making their expression an ongoing part of their lives.

So they saw this Gettysburg battlefield roll into lush new folds in 1900.

Many were at ease with their work.

The wealthier spent a day in the country.

Americans also expected to add their own personal ties to those structures. Besides just finding some enjoyment and pleasure through the clear obvious parts of their society, like their work or class, they made the sheer satisfying pleasure of being with one another add a layer of expression to their structures.

Children enjoyed meeting Madame Schumann-Heink.

Harry S. Truman and Eleanor Roosevelt breakfasted at the Democratic Convention in 1952.

More, they combined these two different kinds of contentment into a complete style, tone, and desire and made *it* become the nub of their lives. It wasn't that they found an expressive form for their lives through their work, then turned around to create another through their personal attachments; but rather that they let the one that streamed through their structures and the other that rambled through their personal ties combine into a blooming core of contentment from which they expected future deeds, actions, and new forms to grow.

So this family posed for its portrait in the 1880s by standing in front of its house and including the cows, horses, plows, and the level grass and open sky.

But they *used* the sky. They used that blasted interminably-moving glob of indefinable space as part of their portrait. And it wasn't a beautiful romantic sky that they used, either, but a flat toneless range that had no beginning and no end. Making it stand with all those clearly established toe holds they had managed to accrue in their lifetime, they settled it right into their portrait. They settled the space that sifted between their delineated specific achievements and the space that drifted beyond those right and proper symbols into clearly established places. We all know that Americans flourished in using and adapting their society's structures. But they also stretched their vision to move into the not yet definable. And to give that undefinable range of possibilities a firm footing.

No great wonder, then, that thirty years later, they made room for all the obtuse new shapes that were to come with the technological age, that they saw air ships in their vision of that open sky, and that they saw the many diverse shapes of air

ships in their conception of what a blooming profuse life was all about.

As if there were no limits. As if they could mix anything together—upset lives, change ways, add unknowns—and always produce a better life. Experimenting with a tumbling mass of sometimes definable and often intangible forms, they mixed people, things, and inventions into new and different patterns. Experimenting, they created. Moreover, in the process of experimenting and creating they extended the dimensions with which they lived and thought.

So they extended this racing car into a drawn-out design...

...devised makeshift arrangements to get from a seaplane that just landed in water to the surrounding embankments...

...and played with the idea of seeing a woman change a tire. Though laughing at the fact that she was, they also thought of her with that car and indeed changing its tire.

It was fun to think of how much one could stretch the limits of one's life, of how much one could draw the instruments one used and the satisfactions one experienced into the possibilities one expected to build. Incorporating delicate respect with intangible expression and lining them up with natural and mechanical certainties, a person used each part of his life as if it were a tool in his command, as if he could control each as he came to control more. Then extending himself through those tools, he made his own life richer at the same time he made his whole rambling use of technology human. He made his tools come to life in the same way he did.

Much of this grew out of Americans' conception of themselves as craftsmen in the early nineteenth century, men in the bottoming room of this shoe factory assuming a certain domain over their work even though they worked in a factory.

It continued into the latter part of the century, these women branding cattle after having dressed for the photographer.

It even continued into the middle of the twentieth century, as this stonemason sat in front of his work as if it was his own, though it was actually part of the organizational scheme that built the Empire State Building...

...while this man directed the actual placement of beams in the construction of that building.

Workers don't sit in front of their work as that stonemason did anymore. Women don't lose themselves so completely to their jobs, especially after they get dressed for the photographer. And we don't see a construction worker who is so much a person on the job that he squints to let his pleasure help place the beam.

Americans used to assume that the possibility of controlling their lives was real. They set out across the country, greeted the railroad and telegraph's arrival, and watched lacy steel buildings rise in their cities. They expected the new tangible gains all around them were ways they could adapt to more fully controlling their lives. They became people of quiet but greater conviction. It was just easy and natural to know that everything would work.

So Caroline Pico and Maria Dominguez sat for the camera in 1850.

Pascual Marquez' bathhouse spread onto the Santa Monica beachfront and opened itself to include a flag, a variety of people, and different modes of dress and means of travel...

...while Mr. Whitmore and his workers stood squarely in front of their shop as they moved obliquely through the space around them.

It wasn't only that Americans controlled their machines and the technology the machines brought. They also expected to control the most everyday elemental things they did in the morning, noon, and night, like where they would work, how they would live, and what kind of life they would choose—even those personal aspects that ran tangentially off the question of work, like being black, wanting peace, and living as an old person. Of course we know that Americans didn't fully and,

in some instances, never even partially, create that power, that they violently broke out of restraints in the nineteenth and twentieth centuries in the attempt to create some of that power. But we also know that in visualizing and thinking with the possibilities of creating that control, Americans created a wholeness about their lives that they used.

These wives of strikers protested against the arrest of Mother Jones, a radical who came to speak to their striker husbands in the Trinidad mines in Colorado in 1913.

The parents of Imogen Cunningham, the photographer, sat for a portrait with their cow and bucket in 1923.

This sharecropper stood with a fiery range of pleasures and dissatisfactions.

Americans had learned to confront adverse situations. More than accepting restraint or bowing to more superior powers, they faced head-on what they assumed to be the facts of their existence.

So they faced death. This child died about 1845.

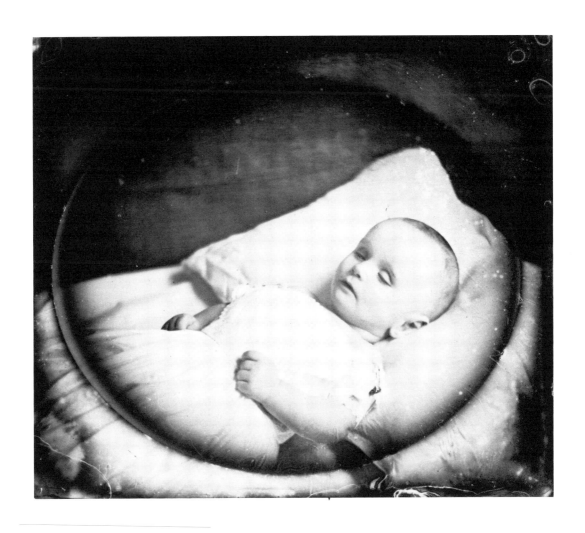

Up until World War II Americans essentially assumed that they could meet and incorporate whatever came their way. Regardless of the particular conflicts they might face in each period of time, Americans assumed that they could absorb all they confronted and turn it into a new realm of expression. It wasn't that they expected to be victorious and down all opposition, but rather that they could sweep those conflicting up-

setting discrepancies into an ever enlarged conception of the new and future life, that just as they could create with all of those delights and inventions so could they create with anything that jarred them. They drew the conflicts of their times and the soothing self-satisfying ways they had fashioned into a relaxed but explorative search.

So they met out on the streets of Maunch Creek, Pennsylvania, in 1940...

...scrambled up the summit of McClellan's Mountain in the 1880s...

...and turned a tenement house bathroom into a smiling part of their lives.

Some stood with gutsy triumph in front of a mill they didn't own and couldn't expect to.

Another jumped with a disregard for the place around...

. . . while another strode through a break in the movement of World War II.

People even thought that the whole mass of inefficient by-products—wading through knee-deep water, becoming a share-cropper, fighting a war—could help produce that more human existence. It was possible to think of how one would make the spin-offs and extras stand with the basic, of how one could make the counterpoints stand with the productive capacities that unraveled them—make each part of each fact add to their conception of a more satisfying life. There was still room, even through the end of World War II.

When this soldier entered liberated Paris in 1945 mounted on a U.S. Army tank he broke into the stretch of emotions that many felt in realizing a triumph that came from victory in World War II but that also symbolized a human triumph for the mid-twentieth century.

Americans often don't like to use the words "human expression," as if the words are too soft for the hard, nose-to-the-grindstone feelings they have about the lives they lead, as if ways filled with that expression couldn't possibly be successful. Instead they jag up their thoughts with images of successful men riding roughshod over satisfying experiences, as if adventure was opposite to personal satisfaction and could never include such satisfyingly comfortable notions.

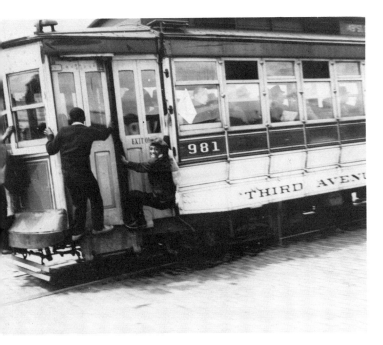

But adventure was of the same ilk. It grew within the same parameters as that softer mode of expression we now set outside of those limits. When these men and women boarded the train they bustled about. They moved, shoved, and laughed while the woman with the camera used a new piece of technology to shove that delight further. It's not as if we don't have fun with the camera today. We fuss with it, love it, but however we use it we never let it unbalance what we expect. We never let it shake up or change the mood and character of our lives. When this woman used the camera she jarred the scene and changed its perspective. She used a new piece of technology to prod boundaries and build delight.

In a quieter vein this family stood in front of the dugout they first built, the lean-to they added, and the full complete house the whole family built over a period of twenty years.

Kids who lived in New York City hooked a ride from a trolley in the 1930s . . .

. . . laughing figures jumped off the brick wall of a city stoop . . .

. . . and Julia Clark sat in the calm of her plane as she was about to test-drive it in 1911. It failed.

Americans expected to be successful and they moved with a confidence that was sometimes exuberant and sometimes calm. But where we appreciate success by thinking of it in terms of achieving certain goals, earlier Americans experienced success in the process of bringing an adventurous search to fruition. It was satisfying to create. And that was success.

More, without consciously singling out space, they nonetheless used it and used it as if it were alive and real and the next step in their thoughts. Though we might look at the space around Julia Clark or the family and its house and think it was empty, they assumed it was real and substantive, a means by which they fiddled with ideas and moved and thought and explored. For while we see little room for expansion today and don't light up to possibilities even when space offers them, they saw the many faces and shapes of space and construed them all as possible avenues of exploration. Space was an entity. Further, through it they could reach into unknowns and produce new satisfactions and successes.

So these men and women dipped into this cave in the 1890s . . .

. . . while these children moved through a hush of rocks between La Jolla and Alligator Cove along the Pacific Coast.

Harnessing space to their conception of technology, they used planes and space to spell each other off, planes dipping them further into space as space more fully opened new realms of technology. Nature and science were two sides of the same coin, not opposite fields of interest.

Far from the way we ride in a feelingless jet, for instance, and layer ourselves off from space, this man flew over San Diego in 1939 and made the space around him come to life. It was immediate and real and personal. His head stuck right into it and he expected to realize a certain fulfillment through it. To think of him conquering space is out of kilter. He was extending himself through it, becoming part of it. Unlike the way we separate ourselves from the possibilities it offers, he was creating with it.

In the same vein this woman sat back in a car that passed in front of the War Department Building in Washington in 1905, the lines and design of the building making the space she used come to life.

When Americans built towns in the nineteenth century they used space with that same live conception. Transforming it into units they could almost touch, these men in Williams, Arizona, stood up and down the length and breadth of this railroad, in effect becoming tools that marked space off into human units.

Those who built Miles City, Montana, made the buildings into tools, any two buildings holding a unit of space between them that one could almost touch . . .

... while some, even as late as the 1950s, still conceived of themselves exploring landed space adventurously, such as this man on a tractor on a farm in the Black Hills of South Dakota.

Some lived more simply.

These upper-class women had fun with their children in Central Park, New York City, in 1896.

The professor's family celebrated his birthday with a silly lovely snowman as a guest of honor in California in the 1890s.

This boy seemed to love obeying his teacher and the health rules she taught him at Ethical Culture's elementary school in New York City in the 1930s...

... while these children sang in a Sunday school chorus in Penderlea Homesteads, North Carolina, in 1937.

At the same time Americans lived adventurously they also developed very personal kinds of satisfaction with the things they did...

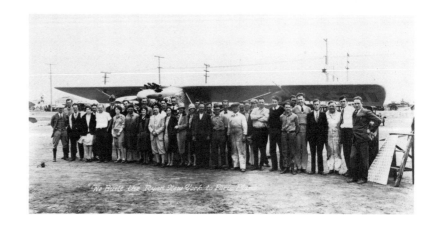

... then turned them into the sense of what a community was and how they belonged to it. It was the most natural thing in the world for Americans to support a union organizer and rile against the squealer who kept that union from coming to fruition, such as this committee organizing a miner's union in the Colorado lead mines in 1913 ...

... and for these workers to become a community in building Charles Lindbergh's plane that flew the Atlantic in 1927 in the same way that those who organized a union in 1913 developed their community.

Developing a community and realizing personal success were intimately bound to each other. One enlarged the meaning of the other.

These women met together for the afternoon.

These men and women danced during their lunch hour.

As each of these men weighed up the fish and packaged it for sale, they worked with each other. Though expressing some of the work's frustrations, they also built its pace and satisfactions.

Letting go, these men tied themselves to the success of World War II. Having achieved distinction for speed, efficiency, and quality of work because they poured concrete for twenty-four igloos in twenty-four hours, each man felt as if he himself helped bring about the triumph of the war and its purpose.

Americans used to feel a part of some grand enlarged scheme of life at the same time they saw, felt, and imagined themselves becoming more singularly satisfied. More, they imagined that the combination of personal success and enlarged community would only become a wellspring, that out of some central source they could continue to produce the human dimensions they expected. As if there was such a thing as a regenerative supply of life, and it was the same as the texture of life itself.

Sometimes adults tried to make their politics speak with that profuse sense of creating new life, as are these men and women sweeping around Adlai Stevenson in 1952 when he ran for President.

Sometimes Americans saw that profusion in a lush array of products, such as in this cheese store in Greenwich Village in 1937.

Sometimes kids lined themselves up and multiplied themselves into a mass that didn't yet ask them to conform, as occurred in San Diego in 1937.

Not that everybody thought he would produce that continuous
profusion of life himself. It was just that it was still possible
to think that someway, somehow one could break out of the
limits within which one lived and set up new ties and weave
the most connected satisfying society, that the process of
creating that more perfect society was still real.

They saw roads and rivers wind into mountains, as in this
view of Pittsburgh, and felt the continuous unpredictable
energy and power they might produce. They saw that energy
and thought of it as a fountain of life.

So they conceived of such constantly flowing energy generating
a more beautiful society, as if profusion and beauty necessarily
ran with each other, as if the more perfect society they were
sure they could produce had to be beautiful.

They saw these oil tanks sitting in the glow of the sun, the calculable fact of productive life carrying the germ of beauty within its patterns.

Some walked through the brightly lit mellowed life of a city street in the 1920s.

Others saw the beauty of one hundred years ago.

The point was that up to the 1950s Americans still dreamed. Not in a fantasizing way but in a way that made them think their future could be productive, beautiful, and most of all have its own regenerative sources. Instead of shrinking from uncertainties they slid into a frame of mind that allowed them to harness one stream of life to another and imagine the beauty, bounty, and unpredictable future their new technology would produce—and see it as a life of greater human texture. It was still possible for them to think their new technology would take them closer to that more perfect society, to the brink of a new realm of life that would generate its own calm but excitement.

So they stood on a ledge with their cars ready to make their future unfold.

Illusions

During these same years life in America also started to collapse. For even though girls in the broom factory built satisfactory circles of life, and Julia Clark looked as if she was sitting on top of the world before test-driving her plane, and all those men and women scrambled about the train station as if they owned it, others doubted more than ever that life could become that blooming happy in America.

This boy stood outside his home in 1912...

...while these women sat in front of a mission in California in 1900.

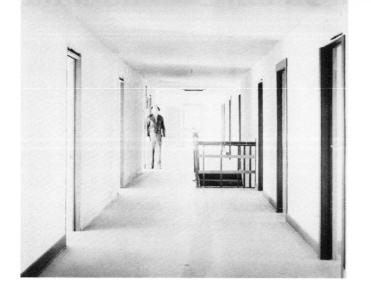

Where was the effusive productive community they expected to build? The Borego Hotel looked bleak in 1938.

Disquiet rumbled through this group in Camp Kearney, California, in 1918 . . .

. . . and these men became a disconnected fumble watching a medicine show.

The satisfaction with which blacks and whites rode this Louisville bus was far from the fulfillment Americans had achieved when they confronted and met situations head-on.

By 1970 one could laugh and live in a profuse room yet have the eerie feeling that however more filled that room became it could never offer new life, that all of its happiness was tied to the forms that people had created and stopped creating, that it was empty of new possibilities while maintaining the decency of the old.

For apart from the doubt and disquiet Americans experienced, they began to accept the way their lives ran. They began to move with the patterns that circled about them as if they didn't have much choice—and why choose, anyway. Weren't they content? They had a roof over their heads. And weren't they living with some of the rock-bottom values they could hold dear to their hearts and know would never vanish? At least they could work and earn a living and go about their business. Americans turned away from meeting either pain or fulfillment head-on. They rather simply accepted the way their lives ran.

So this boy worked, neither angry nor triumphant.

These farm people in California stood next to the shack in which they lived, the rocky soil from which they tried to grow crops spread around them.

Even when life seemed to grow bleak they accepted its patterns and kept their feelings to themselves. This man and girl walked down a railroad track in the 1880s.

They avoided conflicts, let a dehumanizing damper settle over their lives, and resigned themselves to the fact they would have to live life the way it ran. They began to feel they should not experience satisfaction, that they didn't have a right to want fulfillment, that it was their lot in life to live simply with what they had. There was nothing they could or should do about it.

These women sat on the porch of their cabin waiting for the Norris Dam waters from the Clinch River to fill up their valley. Part of the Tennessee Valley Authority redevelopment program, it brought a "good" into a depressed area. But these people weren't creating their lives. They were rather waiting for it to take shape. They were silent accompanists to others' use of power.

By 1970 many lived with an emptiness they didn't create.

Structured, adequate, and hugging that whole middle ground, it prevented one from entering, injecting, and creating one's

own. Americans began to accept what they called the fate of their lives. At the same time that Americans continued to think they could expand the meaning and scope of their lives, many took little satisfaction from what they could do.

These blacks made snuff in Richmond, Virginia, after the Civil War . . .

. . . while this quartet and performer accepted a skimmed shiny reflection of fun rather than one they could build—either out of the car or their own lives.

Fifty years later this woman rattled around next to the glitter the car brought.

Americans started to live on the periphery of lives they might have created. Reduced to being satisfied with a glint of happiness or a glimmer of success, they let themselves walk in the

patterns others produced as if their lives were only to reflect others' triumph, as if they were to experience no triumph themselves. Submitting to the powers that be, they also began changing the hopes they had constructed for themselves through their technology.

Where they had used their machines to help them explore they now began emulating a machine because it wouldn't. It substituted less human effort for the risky provocative effort they had used. They saw the relief it brought. They saw it siphon off work and drain away the expendable moves they never minded making as long as they felt they might produce a better life but which they now doubted they could. Americans put aside the fun they had had in using a machine when its results were unpredictable and began feeling a mild fat satisfaction in seeing a machine hammer out a successful course.

This man stood in the lineup of the machine's power.

Thirty years later a man looked machine-like.

Americans had respected machines because they were like people. Now they began to love their machines because they weren't and had less and less smack of a human hand in what they did.

This car was getting ready to turn right into Louisville in 1921 . . .

. . . while those watching this balloon saw the strings operating the flight.

Americans began to love the pieces and offshoots of technology they were producing. More, they looked to their buildings with the same gimmicky delight and overawed sense of magnificence. For if machines were a part of the great new society, the new high-rising steel structures they could build with their more perfectly wrought steel represented the technological society's greater strength and increasing power. It seemed silly, for instance, to think of the Empire State Building as a force growing out of the personal adventure men put into its steel and stone. It was a great new giant, a marvelous new prop with which to see success and glitter.

One could even mask the adventure others put into such creation. Just seal off its life. Veil its greatness. Drape it in mystery. With no apparent connection to the human stresses and desires that built them, these grain elevators stood in the filmy light that celebrated success rather than in the clear sparkle of light that might open the processes that created them.

By 1970 Americans lived with illusions of success as if they were the very essence of success itself. They saw their technology draped in marvelous deeds and phenomenal output. And whether they hated the fact that this is what they now called success or emulated the strength and power it brought, they saw their technology, especially their cars, connected to that success and power. Technology as a human force was outmoded. It had no connection to the "real" world.

No longer expecting their technology to help them triumph, they skirted around the issues that produced conflict and lived with any of the tangents such conflict produced. Glory? Why not. Fury? If there was enough fight. The important thing was that it didn't matter to which tangent they attached themselves as long as one felt the power it might bring.

While they withdrew. There was no room for human involvement in such a conception. A person was an instrument. So these men and women stood on the fringes of the motorcycle race neither drawing closer nor running from it. As if they were immune to the horrors and joys of the race but delighted with the fury of power, they set the stage for themselves becoming onlookers to the power they had once created and stood transfixed rather than involved with the energy the race produced while echoing the fury it let fly.

Seeing their new technological society as units of power, Americans began to welcome the way that power shaped their new mass society. The variety they had built out of a machine's individuality was no longer useful. It didn't increase power and it got in the way of those trying to extend the machine's.

Rather than relish such a prickly mixed bag of delight as they did at that air show in 1910 or feel the fun the kids had at that Saturday afternoon movie, they turned to admire the solid band of strength that this first mass air flight over San Diego brought in 1918. Where they had earlier had fun with quirks . . . and created strength and power out of divergencies, they now began to soften those edges and shape divergent directions into the most solid mass they could.

Solid strength counted, not all those lovable different directions that suggested the many diverse possibilities that one could still call upon or hope to activate. When workmen lined themselves up at a Norris Dam construction site in 1933 they turned themselves into a solid mass of people far different from the construction workers at the Empire State Building site who let individual characteristics spill off their work. Each of these men was also much less a whole complete person than the worker in the bottoming room of the B. F. Spinney shoe factory.

The human values that Americans had constructed out of their workday, had extended into their communities, and had expected to produce with their uses of technology had begun to break down. Factory workers and immigrants began to feel the pain more than the effusive productive life they had expected to create in that new industrial society.

These girls finished their workday at the Richmond Hosiery Company in Roseville, Georgia, in 1910.

This woman shopped in Hester Street in New York in 1898.

This man walked through San Francisco.

Pain increased in the 1930s when a depression further dammed up hopes and the illusion of waiting and thinking something might happen because one waited added to that pain. Would anything happen? Could it? Hanging between the possibilities that one might still create one's society and the despair of seeing those possibilities vanish, Americans thought they might change something if they could move while they waited.

Migrant packinghouse workers waited for work at this railroad station in Belle Glade, Florida.

This unemployed fur trapper seemed ready to break through the pain that surrounded him in Placquemarine Parish, Louisiana.

Today pain has settled into American lives, as if there was no point in even trying to upset its hold, as if one is to accept its place, and like this woman, let it spread out into the quietest corners of one's life.

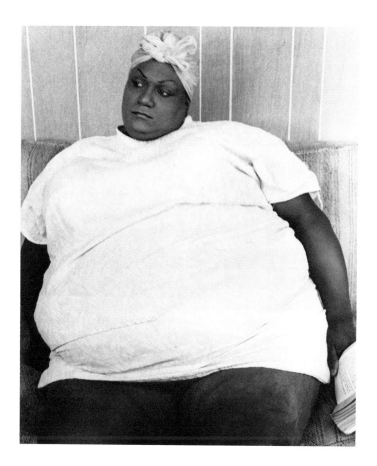

For there was shiny cool fun to be had in American life. Never mind the fun that kids who explored the cove between La Jolla and Alligator Cove had or those who hooked a ride from the Third Avenue trolley in New York had. Forget about the fun one could create by uprooting life and turning it into new units of space, new conceptions of work, or new communities. Americans wanted a shiny glittering surface of fun. They made themselves into stick figures that played with surfaces, then molded those figures into a mass.

This is the crew of the *U.S.S. Saratoga* in 1912.

These girls danced at the Christmas party that the Ryan Aircraft Company gave at Lindbergh Field in San Diego in 1936.

These women held pigeons imported from Canada.

Others poured a mouth-watering goodness into the trees they lined up in Balboa Park, California, in 1915, then nestling into the comfort of ornate Mediterranean balconies, they settled onto a skimmed thin surface of superficialities and a fat blown-up dream of lushness.

More, they constructed a shiny new city outside of Los Angeles, combining a halfhearted Utopian desire with that skinny image of ventureless satisfaction, and called it Venice. Letting gondoliers skim through waters, they never changed the substance of their life on shore . . .

. . . built a storybook-like setting for an amusement center just a few years before and a few miles away from what was to become Hollywood . . .

. . . and watched Maggie remind everyone of the outsized appetites for fun all could have.

As the twentieth century moved on, Americans responded to the call of the celebrity. Although they had earlier flocked to see the race of horses or cars at a track, now they moved over to the slightest dip in the leg that Dorothy Lamour so satisfyingly exhibited at Del Mar Racetrack . . .

Maggie at Venice Cal.

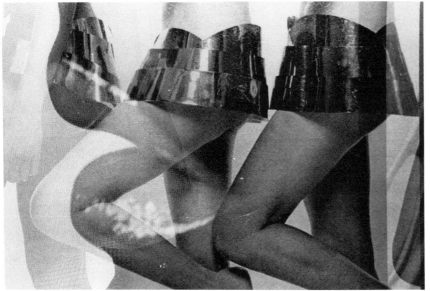

...then used sex to sell all those glistening smooth soft chewy fruits...

...and by 1970 let soft chewy adornments become jagged edges that flicked across a screen.

Of course Americans have always had a double-hung attitude toward women. Though at one with the women who confronted Mother Jones' arrest in 1913, they also stripped women of a range of personal desires and wants. Like the way Americans dehumanized adventure and turned mechanical devices into nonhuman instruments of power so did they begin thinking of women as instrumental parts of their society, as buttons, bells, and switches they could turn off and on.

When Mrs. Mark Lewis rode through this crowd in Pasadena in 1896, she filled one of the slots on that instrumental panel as Queen of the Rose Festival.

Eighty years later this young girl was learning how to fill a similar role.

DIXIE SLEEPER

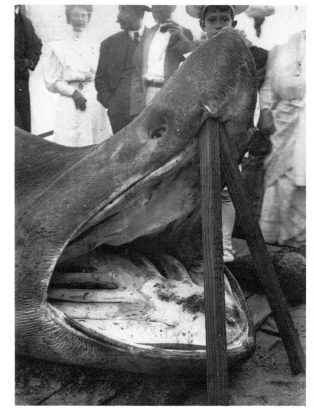

So was it easier to squeeze the life out of other areas of thought. Why search for causes? It was a waste of time. Americans developed panaceas to cure everything. If little children couldn't play with pretty soft animals in the wilderness they could visit and play with fake animals. This little girl stands in Woodward's Gardens in San Francisco in the 1880s.

When crops died in the San Fernando Valley in the 1890s and many were sure that rabbits ate those crops right from their roots, they went on a mass rabbit hunt and strung up dead rabbits for everyone to see how singularly happy they could be with that victory.

If a man didn't sleep well at night he could buy a better bed, and decide which by measuring his weight against a barrel's, as here in the 1920s.

Anyway, American animals were bigger, better, and bolder than any other and could always take the edge off life. This alligator's mouth was propped open in 1910.

The lions and statuary in this antique shop in New York on Third Avenue come alive.

But it was a holding action. It was all a last-ditch stand against the disintegration of expression that was setting in, a way of Americans trying to prevent themselves from seeing the decay. It was as if by standing with make-believe animals when real ones provided excitement, propping a mouth open to show that adventure still existed, and testing mattresses to prove one's individuality that they could show that nothing was different, that they could still have fun with rambling experimental runs. It was as if they could tell themselves that life wasn't running downhill, that illusions were happiness and that panaceas fixed what was going wrong.

The point was that Americans accepted those panaceas and illusions as ways out of the maze that was closing them in, as devices they could use to lift some of their disappointment. After all, in the late nineteenth century they had learned to use clear specific codes with proven results when they spent a social afternoon in upper-class company, or if they were children reciting their lessons in school. Couldn't they use the same narrow system of thinking in everything they did? Didn't everyone, for instance, love his country? They didn't really need to show the range and nuances of that expression. Seeing one tree was the same as seeing them all. All they needed was to set up some rules, then follow them without wavering, certainly without letting anything so slight as a thought or feeling clutter their minds.

This woman served her country by manning the telephones while men were away at war.

These men in an Army camp during World War I set flags about them.

One of these girls spearheaded a glamorous turn on the waters of San Diego Bay with the American flag.

Assuming themselves to be less than the people who once expected to create their lives, they accepted the fact that the instrumentality of their society would create their societal

organizations. In effect they gave up the possibilities they had always held onto of controlling and determining the course of their lives.

GLORIETTA
SAN DIEGO

Some, as far back as the turn of the century, accepted the fact of living next to oil wells.

Others submitted the observance of Easter morning to the celebrity-laden image of bright lights and shiny new fun, as here at Mount Davidson in California.

Even when John L. Lewis, head of the United Mine Workers in the 1940s and 1950s, enabled his union members to think with the personal satisfactions they wanted, he turned out to look like the mob around him, as if he would squelch anything that interfered with his course regardless of its worth.

Meanwhile, some still tried to make the essential strands of their different lives find a new meeting ground. This govern-

ment agent, white farmer, and black farmer tried to talk to each other in the 1920s.

But a dead triangle occupied that center space, a dead empty space that kept one man away from the other, each behind lines, and one unconnected to another. Americans lost the belief that they could step out from the structure that maintained their lives and succeed in building a more expressive life. They lost their sure footing, the belief that somehow they would build a more creative life even as they tumbled and fell into new problems and greater disorder. It wasn't that they backed away from newly broken-down forms or even that those newly broken-down forms swamped their lives, but rather that there seemed little hope of ever building that belief again.

The life that this former plantation house once exuded was lost. More, it seemed impossible to think of constructing new life from within its shell.

In the 1930s people who waited for the elevated train in New York didn't look at all like those who scrambled about the station waiting for the Mount Washington Railroad...

... while those who rode the subway and read of President Franklin D. Roosevelt's death in 1945 felt the end of an era in American life. Americans had believed that victory in World War II would increase the human dimensions of their lives. They had also looked to FDR's leadership as a way of supporting their belief that it was still possible to tie one's individual desires for greater expression to the fuller national aims of

the country. That that notion had been eroding didn't matter so much as that it was still possible to believe that in fighting World War II Americans could come a step closer to national and personal fruition, that however threadbare those last strands of belief were, they were still real. They saw their own greater contentment tied to the victory FDR would bring and when he died, so soon after that victory was won, they felt wiped out. As if it could never be. As if such human triumph was lost and no longer possible.

Many saw themselves as used up as this man sitting in front of the Fulton Fish Market in the 1930s.

Some identified with Mr. Whittley who visited his general store in Wendell, North Carolina, in 1939 and was also president of the town's bank—not so much for the way he commandeered his store, but for the way he sat above the problems that ran around him. It wasn't that they admired the hard-dealing boss-of-a-town look he had, but that he looked as if he wouldn't think of engaging himself with any of the elements that pushed him up front.

Others saw themselves as submissive as these men watching a medicine show in Huntingdon, Tennessee.

Some muted their feelings into a fun show. This was in
Klamath Falls, Oregon, in 1942.

Still others tried to bypass their present and think of some silken glorious pools that would shine and reflect well upon their lives, of that point in time when they wouldn't have to worry about triumph but only cast themselves into a permanent unchanging die. It was as if they couldn't gain life out of their mortality and turned to the hazy image of a monumentalized future as the saving grace for having lived, as if they needed to turn to a lifeless reminder of what was once possible, as if everything about their mortal lives was used up.

This monument was built to Douglas Fairbanks, Sr., in 1941 . . .

... while this stood at the Panama Pacific Exhibition in 1915 when many began to settle back into such institutionalized mirrors.

For these were the real new mirrors of American life, the kinds of successes for which most Americans began to hope. Americans began to want their success to shine with the glitter they saw in the moonlight of their romance with their productive capacity. But most of all they wanted it to shine with the glitter of the brightest triumph, even though they never wanted to let go of the other dreams. But did.

Illusions and Realities All Used Up

Was America this used up? Could only a slightly wacky woman show a love for her country? Was that what America had come to mean? How different from 1943 when this other woman spilled out of her wackiness by going to feed the pigeons in Lafayette Park in Washington, D.C., each day for thirteen years.

Our flag-kissing woman picked symbols and signs that had evolved from tight America—the glittering faces, sunlit flowers, bright shiny flag, and smoothed-down look of each and every President over the past twenty years, each one looking much the same as the other, the whole mess of parts from Ike to JFK as indistinct from each other as the fragments they were of the American experience and what it might have been. For more than walking through the bleakness of a railroad, avoiding the dehumanized state of factory life, absorbing the mute sunniness of a shack, or trying to grow crops from worn-out soil, by the 1960s a person separated himself from even those ways. None of them would work. They were all used up. It's not that the fruitful possibilities in American life wouldn't work, but that the negative thrusts from which one had come to extract a morsel of contentment were all used up.

In the 1870s, for instance, Americans had begun to think with the idea of monumentality. Using wealth and design to see their cities through a lens that abstracted strength and distorted power, they produced a monumentality they found perfectly satisfactory.

But where that monumentality shoved them onto a ledge of
possibility in the nineteenth century, they felt its blown-up
decay by 1970.

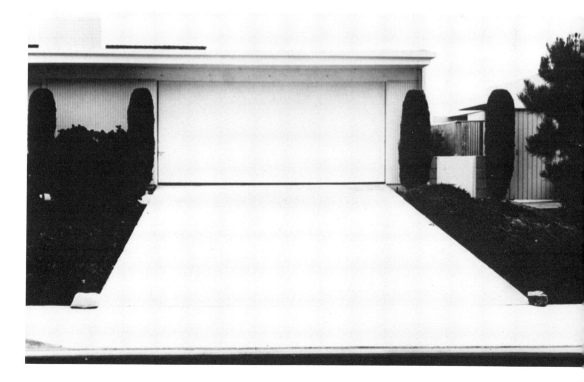

So too where some had found a sense of triumph through peripheral realms of adventure in the same turn-of-the-century years, they found it empty of triumph by 1970.

Americans could no longer conceive of monumentality as expression. Nor could they be satisfied with the watered-down triumph they had experienced through illusory realms. They could no longer tell themselves that glitter would relieve, that success would palliate, and that substitutes were real. Though Americans produced sweeping illusions and grand hopes and lived by and with them one hundred years ago, they couldn't do that by 1970.

More, they let the new dehumanizing patterns incorporate a person into their very shape and design. A machine could softly and unobstrusively wrap a person into its life. No great slam-bang container to wipe out human expression. Just a smooth quiet flick of the wrist. You could just turn the machine around, then upside down, and there was no person. It just happened; no one planned it.

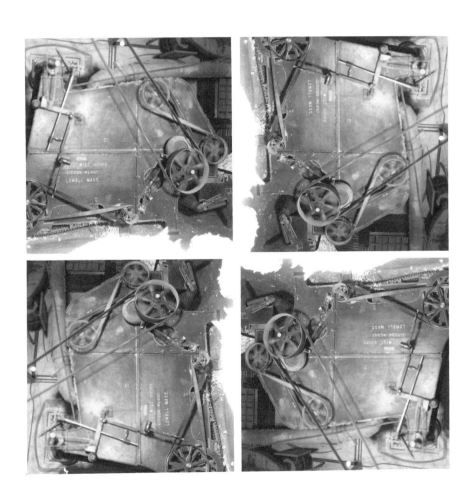

For Americans began to resign themselves to the overhauling sweep of a power they assumed they could not confront. Whether old or young they began to think of themselves having nothing to say or do about the course of their lives. Where they saw the mute silent life existing somewhere out there earlier in the century, by 1970 they assumed that they themselves were the patterns that had formerly existed out there. It wasn't that the old were worn out but rather that old and young were now becoming part of the patterns that stripped a person of life.

So this silk worker seems to have given up in the same way this young person is becoming his stick-figure image . . .

. . . while these three sat on a lawn after riots in 1967. Neither fulfilled nor energized, content nor worked up, they were at one with the destruction around them.

Did Americans have any choices? Could they strike out on any path? Was everyone frozen? In this civil rights demonstration the policeman, using the decent values he had absorbed from American life, could do no other than use them to preserve his tightly constrained America. The dog did as he was trained . . . and the people were backed into a motionless state. The boy, of course, was cornered. Unlike child laborers in the early part of the century who either sidestepped the dehumanizing swell of their factory or confronted it with gutsy triumph, this boy could do neither. He had no choices. He couldn't choose to triumph or not. Nor could he build illusions out of personal expression or hang on an image of grand glittering mirrors. All those avenues were closed off.

More, Americans assumed that living a dehumanized life was normal and okay and perfectly all right and acceptable. In fact, fine good clean American fun. They began to love the languid ways and fluid movement and like these kids on a California beach melted right back into the very form and shape of the machines themselves, both they and their machines less than the people they once expected both they and their machines to be.

Where the car trolley and people were all parts of a happy
confusion in a crazy accident in Washington, D.C., in 1925—
obviously an accident in which those silly machines didn't
yet know they weren't to behave as human tools, by 1970
Americans didn't have such silly thoughts about their cars.
Cars human? Sounds dumb. Machines are instruments of
power. They're shiny and new and when they aren't they break
down and become nothing ...

... like this sheriff's car ablaze in California in 1969.

However angry anyone was in 1925 they would not burn a car. It could still take one to the ledge of what might be, let one think of how much one could create and shape his life. It still held too many possibilities. In the same way, even though many lived with dismembered parts of their existence piled high, as in this store-front window in the 1930s, they still expected to get their lives in shape. Though they floundered with no jobs, often moved aimlessly about, and felt the pain of a depression, they still expected they could transform their broken-up lives into a whole existence. Dismembering didn't produce despair. Americans expected to overcome it. That wasn't so by 1970.

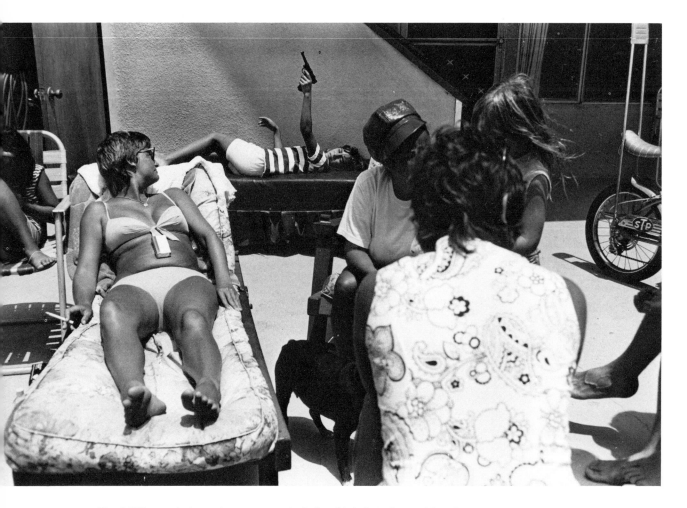

By 1970 most Americans accepted the disjointed rumble about them as the most normal thing in the world. They even told themselves they were having fun, living a good life, suffering little, owning cars and planes, and able to settle into the pleasures of the good life they saw around them. They nestled back into their chairs, lived disconnected, sunny, chaotic lives and loved it. This is in Balboa, California.

Did Americans really accept such a cut-up state of existence?
Did they live as disjointed and disconnected, as untied to any
other person or thing as all that?

In 1940, when a man was murdered on the streets of New York,
people stood about. They didn't do very much, but they gathered
around and came close and if they were glued to the pavement
they at least felt tied enough to the man to stay around and be
part of the scene. They didn't know what to do but they belonged and they stayed.

In 1970, after the riots in East Los Angeles and two lay dead in
the street, no one came close. Everyone scattered. Didn't inter-
fere. Didn't get involved. Too risky.

Sometimes consciously, often unconsciously, Americans accepted this ripped-open state of existence. They assumed that this was what life was all about, that that's the way Americans lived. They cut off whole portions of their lives to stay out of what they would have become a part of in another age.

In fun kids built a stick-figure idol out of making love and the make-believe fun in making love . . .

. . . while in real life people lived the same make-believe half-said life . . . and loved it.

More straightforwardly this woman wore the fun of new America . . .

. . . while this girl lived a life of that fun and began to turn into some of the chaotic moves it spun off . . .

. . . all while Americans began to assume it was perfectly normal to be less than a person, that it was perfectly normal to think one could do nothing about creating his life. The past? Forget it; that's all gone. This is the new hardened-to-America. This is the new technological society that catches glints of the great giant America is to become. A person didn't need to be adventurous; the society and government were strong, even invincible.

And why all that space? A good front lawn was enough, or even an efficient apartment. Then one could sit in the illusion of a luxurious sun and turn on TV to see the image of a new plastic dream. He might even see men on the moon—real stick figures walk through space. A person didn't need to be adventurous. He could live through the movements of the stick figure. That was enough.

Anyway, space was just empty. It offered no excitement and generated no life. As if they had drawn all possible meaning from its reaches, Americans hemmed in their conceptions, shrunk in their society, and pulled in their limits of space. They turned space into a definable item, something one could measure and line up. Deadening such realities as exploring and expanding, Americans replaced the risky adventurous realms they had formerly used with sturdy unflinching facts.

Adventure came to lay in the monkey suit and the robot-like moves, in dehumanizing and wiping out personal satisfaction, not opening it up and increasing it. It lay in less than human capacities and came to have nothing in the world to do with personal satisfaction. And how could anyone think of being powerful enough to structure his life? A stick figure was strong, not a person. How could a person think he even had a right to structure his life?

Both the plainclothesman and the boy accept the fact that they can run down this suspect and strip him as a person, this in New York City.

Men on the floor of the Stock Exchange in New York run as disconnected units between sales . . .

. . . . while the image of what a person might be explodes. A person could no longer think of creating his life so it might become whole. Was he real any more?

By 1970 most Americans lived with great gaping holes and yawning gaps of what their lives might be.

Most of all they lived without the pain of knowing they were destroying their lives. This woman celebrated her birthday in 1964 and said she was having fun. Could Americans truly not know they were experiencing pain? Couldn't they tell the difference between pain and fun? Had American life become that used up?

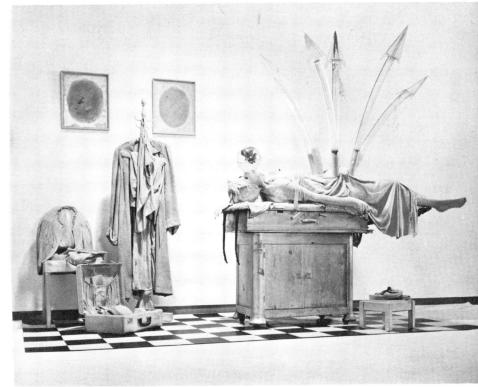

This circus performer in Maryland seemed to ignore the difference between one and the other. More than substituting pain for fun and recognizing the difference between them, he seemed to accept the one for the other and go about his daily business.

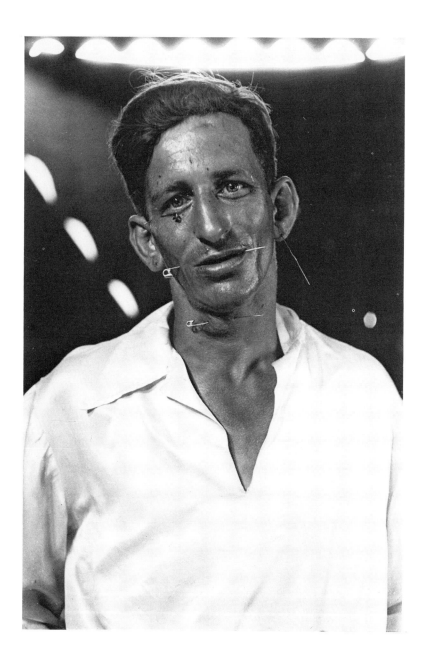

Beyond Used Up America

American life has always flourished because of the expression it fostered. But we can never understand how we've been closed into a choked-off state of existence and why we can't recognize the pain we inflict upon ourselves unless we see how we've expressively used ourselves up. We can never understand why we're used up unless we see how we enlarged our expressive modes without even touching dimensions of freedom.

We've used various forms of expression. One form, blended of economic and social desires, prodded Americans into exploring, then edged up to children who ran between rocks in the nineteenth century and worked in factories and hung off trolleys in the twentieth. Another form showed Americans how to confront issues in the nineteenth century that a variant of that expression taught them how to bypass less majestically in the twentieth. A scientific and cultural form of expression filled the blooming mass of technologically experimental flights that floated through the early twentieth century. A social and economic form lined up American conceptions of success to make success' proliferating possibilities stop; then produce locked-in smoothed-out forms. We know another form of expression as an architectural design that incorporated space into its scope and plan, can trace another through an upper-class graciousness, can even watch another become the contentment with nature that families and children, upper and lower, with and without cars, have always called their own. Americans have used and combined different kinds of expression into everything they have done.

They've also made their expression a fundamental part of their lives, using it to nourish their institutions, resolve their problems, and propel them to new airy reaches. Adapting one form of expression to the time when they waded through knee-deep water from their just-landed seaplane, they used another when they were caught by a depression in Pacquemarine Parish, another when they met out on the streets of Maunch Creek, Pennsylvania, and still another when they tried to substitute glitter for the dimensions of happiness they had once created. They finally substituted pain. Americans drew on their various forms of expression to probe their interiors, think of new possibilities, and build new structures. They even used one or another form to ease them over difficulties. Americans found it easy to rely on their forms of expression, to believe that their expression would flesh out their moves and substantiate their thoughts regardless of what they were doing.

But did Americans become any freer? Because some women spent a lovely afternoon in Louisville and others brought victory home from World War II, did they live any more freely? Were Americans any freer because they opened new ways of expression? Did they become any freer because they devised more exciting, exalting forms of expression? Did they make those ways create new dimensions? Did they expand our conception of freedom? Widen its limits? Deepen its base? Not in the twentieth century.

For a person to live with greater freedom he must consciously expand the ideology by which he lives, then make that conscious expansion a foundation for new acts. At every point of greatness in American life, regardless of the period's simultaneous negative impulses, Americans have expanded the meaning of freedom. They did it in 1776, certainly in the middle of the nineteenth century, even in the Victorian and Industrial conflicts of the 1870s and 1880s.

But in 1913 when the organizing committee for the Colorado Miners' Union fingered a squealer, it essentially backed away from freedom. Calling on decent values that were a part of various American forms of expression, the committee asked the miners to condemn the squealer for threatening those values. Though a few individuals still conceived of freedom as an essential ingredient in their drive for unionization, most miners and employers fought for or against organization on grounds that had nothing to do with freedom. On the one hand miners and employers fought to expand their respective realms

of economic power, while on the other the organizing committee fought to incorporate those commonly decent values into the process of unionization to make those values a surer part of the union man's expression. Miners and owners, union men and not—all expanded their expressive modes but avoided the question of freedom. From the early part of the twentieth century on, Americans have swept decent values into the ongoing patterns of their lives, even changed some of the dominant cultural patterns, but not changed the dimensions of freedom.

This book has been about expression and the various ways it has come to pass in American life, about the overflowing, tangential, halfhearted, even distorted ways it has existed and undermined itself. It also chose to be about expression and not freedom because expression and not freedom has been the common denominator in American life. When the men on the Santa Monica beachfront swelled out along the Pacific, they expressively placed themselves in the patterns and development of their land. When the black quartet and the white children entertained at the auto show in the 1920s, all who moved through that sparkling line-up of glory, whether caught up in the illusion of happiness or just riding its crest, lived more expressively. Even today as families live sunny chaotic lives and can never see the amoebic shape of violence overcoming their soft downy pleasures, and men of business along with strident young break down the wholeness of their lives, everyone still tries to expand the means, ways, and possibilities for expression.

In the last decades we've even made our expressive forms widen the very shape of our culture, actually change the shape of our dominant cultural patterns. Don't we let our modes of dress become more expressive? And doesn't the proliferating swell of art galleries and suburban symphonies, many of them better than our old line institutions, show our dominant cultural patterns widening to take in these expressive forms? Our new expressive forms have become part of our dominant cultural sweep, a grain of the very patterns we use.

But where similar forms preceding them once changed the dimensions of freedom, *they* touched, these don't. We all know how the search for political expression in the years before 1776 created, by the end of the American Revolution, more freedom than colonials had up to that point used. In the same way, we know that the search for human and individual expression in the 1780s, right after the Revolution was over, widened that just-gained freedom to create the hope for a more perfect earthly State, and indeed created the Constitution and the Bill of Rights. We even see how the desire for an individual to realize his own most fruitful state of exisence in the 1870s added a social perspective to accepted conceptions of freedom. But of all the expression that came to pass in the twentieth century, none expanded the freedom with which Americans thought, lived, and acted. Exploration didn't. We hoped technology would. And the move towards a more social state of existence has resulted in no new conceptions of freedom.

Our expressive modes in this last century may even have diminished our conception of freedom. Haven't we been told to watch out for the ways we use our freedom, that it's getting scarce and we should be sure we don't use it up? And don't we accept that admonition, however uneasy it makes us? It's as if we really don't care, as if we believe that as long as we have one or another expressive form at our beck and call, that's all that counts. Americans have always banked on expressing themselves while sidestepping the more basic and fundamental place of freedom, mainly because they've lived with some measure of fruition.

But they don't today. We know our expressive forms are used up. It's not only that freedom has become stagnant but that the life that diverted our attention from that freedom—and palliated our desire for its energy at the same time—has also become stale. We've withdrawn from our cities. We don't let, or more properly, demand that, science open new ways of thinking. We scoff at representation in government. We mute our desires, then become stilled and quiet in the face of giant new choices. Though our dominant culture carries more diverse forms of expression than it ever before managed, we don't think of it supporting our desire for expression. It's as if it can't. No matter how much we hoped the objects and desires that have widened our cultural patterns would swell our expression, they haven't.

These people, for instance, with all of the objects they acquired from living in the mainstream of American culture, stand outside of that culture's framework. They don't use the car, rifle, or any sense of satisfaction to tell us about themselves. They even seem to tell us that all of the accoutrements and ways they acquired couldn't spin off any expression now if they tried. The woman handles a rifle but doesn't look victorious. Both the man and the woman seem to treat the car as a worn-out powerless drag rather than even an instrument of gain; and whether through the absence of sex or the absence of all other spirit, both bypass the radiance and romance that Americans formerly expected from becoming triumphant. Both the man and the woman exist outside of the dominant institutional forms of expression in our society. They also seem to look for different satisfactions, and that veers sharply away from the paths we have taken for the past two hundred years.

From the early nineteenth century until the 1920s American life flowed into an ever-thickening cohesive mainstream. Incorporating differences as it moved through the years, it offered everyone a place in its sweep. Upper or lower, with conscience or without, Americans entered their mainstream society and whether they supported or jarred that ballooning stream, joined it. Critical of that cohesiveness, self-congratulatory of its success, or happily consuming its productive fury, each person expected that his particular desires would make their mark on the whole society, that what he stood for would become part of the society's patterns. Americans believed that their different goals would all reach some sort of fulfillment. In effect they created a texture to American life.

With the 1920s that changed; and from the 1920s until the end of the 1960s Americans set their critical views outside of their main culture's framework but tied themselves to that culture by thinking with its course. No longer believing they could shape its sweep, they nevertheless continued to believe and even more insistently wanted to change its character in some way. Maybe inject it with a new humanist flavor. Perhaps infuse it with hope. At least alter its style. But even in the process of becoming critics Americans never loosened themselves from the mainstream's hold. Measuring their achievement by the way it gave in or stood up, they continued to see the main culture set the terms for their thoughts even though they also stood outside of that culture's sweep. Accepting the name of "counter-culture" they defined themselves in the mainstream's flow, gained their footing by steadying themselves against its direction, then gauged their success by its movement. As if they could change it by standing off but not cut loose from its sweep.

Today, though, many of us doubt we can change that culture and, like the woman with the rifle, live outside of its framework as we seek some form of expression. Drawing upon the color, design, and music that opened new ways of expression and tuned us into the sharp new expressions we might experience in the 1960s, we stopped looking to our dominant culture as the fountain for our future. Regardless of its thickening texture and the swell of new expression it carries, we look outside of its patterns and try to find ways of life unattached to it. There we began to see new forms of expression proliferating on their own account, becoming, in essence, independent units of life gaining momentum and generating their own styles. Of course, in accepting the existence of that independent culture, we also accept the fact that we can create another life with no tie to the dominant one.

But in accepting the existence and strength of our dominant culture on the one hand, then looking to that other life with all of its endless modes of expression on the other, we introduce something new into our life patterns. By accepting but not living by the principles of one stream of life, then building another system of life with no reference points to the established, we're really saying that we accept the schizoid nature of our society as a perfectly normal one, that we assume the only way for anyone to find ways of freeing himself up is through his other self. We assume that a person can go about his business doing all those established normal things, but that his expression will stem from that other self living outside of his proud normal range of accomplishments. We're saying that we assume that an independent other self, moving unconsciously, is blooming. More, that that other self is on equal footing with the self that keeps all those established ways in trim, that our other self tells us as much about our lives and expectations as the proud one, perhaps even what we really want or in which direction we should truly look. It's as if that other self tunes us into the expression we must use while we go about our mainstream lives.

It's not that we're any more or less critical of our dominant culture, or that we accept it or reject it any more than we did fifty years ago. It's rather that we've expanded our dimensions and have found a new place for our other self. It's as if we give our implicit unconscious ways a steadier, more assured place in the spectrum of our lives.

These figures slip from one reality to another as they live between a matter-of-fact mainstream world and an interior one looking for some new form of expression. Swimming through barriers that separate a world of fantasy from what we know to be reality, they allow us to live in both worlds, to stretch our perspective and see the energy and power we might create from each.

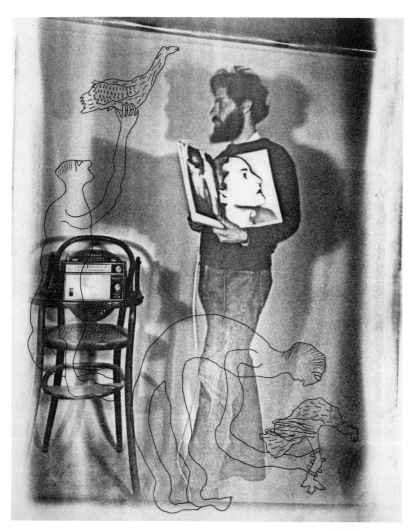

Can we use energy and power from our other selves? We're accustomed to thinking of energy and power coming from our productive mainstream lives, but can we use the rambling modes of expression that belong to our unconscious patterns and make them powerful? Can we make those unconscious ways expand our lives? Not change the structure of our mainstream lives, but become strong in and of themselves? Can we use them as a wedge to force open new ways that we probably cannot even imagine from this vantage point?

If we look at the ways we use space we can get an inkling of how such a notion is possible. Not by looking at the washed clean space that our technologists have lain before us, but by thinking with the space beyond these technologically driven sterilized clean realms. We've seen our expressive forms get used up. If we look at the ways we made space come alive we can get closer to the wishes underlying those forms.

Americans have always used space as a way of saying what they expected to create and what they expected to achieve. When the family stood on the plains with the broom and the cow they let their wide yearning energies spread through their landscape. The men and women who dipped through a cave added a new edge to exploration. Children in school and children in church opened a new easy style. Americans have used space to say how widely, deeply, or effusively they expected to create.

In the same way they've used it to express the dampers that fell over their lives. In the 1920s some mixed a sleazy possibility with their celebration of productive life, at one moment sure of their sumptuous happiness, in the next moment sliding into ways that shrouded their balloon of happiness. It was no accident that this veiled sumptuousness that recognized the glory of production and not the triumph of human development came with the years of the counter-culture, that such sumptuousness was an expression of those who tried to set themselves free from the dominant culture at the same time they tied themselves to it. By 1970 many saw their space becoming as stagnant as their freedom was turning, for even though the spaciousness of the 1870s plain continued to exist in the 1970s house, that spaciousness now hugged all that middle ground and came to a standstill. Spaciousness didn't automatically mean life was going to be great. It also measured fears and halts.

Americans have used space as a way of looking at themselves. Sometimes letting it carry their vision out to the barely perceptible speck on the horizon and making that speck come alive, and sometimes seeing it deaden their most immediate surroundings, Americans have used space to mirror their potential, to show what they were thinking about and if they expected to make their thoughts come to life. Space has always reflected American tremors and desires. It's always shown us what's been getting under our skin and why we've chosen one path over the next. Space has always measured our hopes and the reality we expected those hopes to bring.

Extending ourselves right into its limits—don't we often see our bodies, arms, and legs as part of its scope?—we make our own personal existence become part of its. At times we've even turned it into an inanimate person, discussing our problems with it as we converse with its reach. As if it were a best friend. Americans have used space to say how and if they

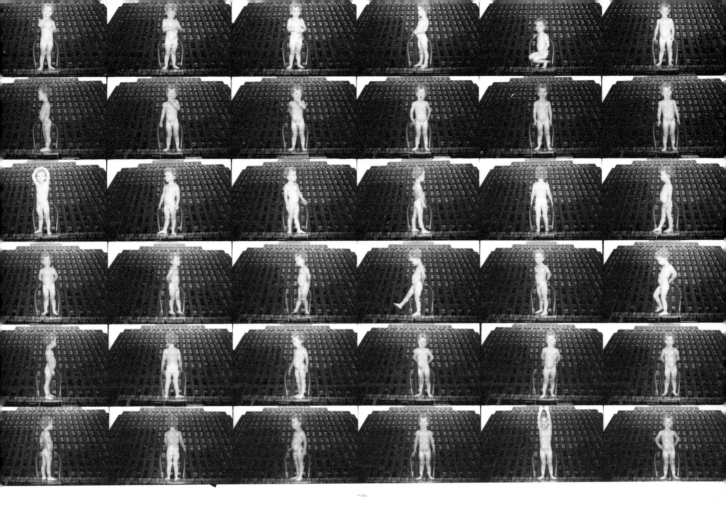

expected to successfully make their own very personal, often inner, human expressions come to life. They've made space speak as an extension of their thoughts, as an active companion of their concerns and expectations.

So the couple who stretches its space and the boy who uses every inch of his continue to do that today. Though one crowds it and the other opens it, both make it take on their personal expressions.

But there's one major new fact. Where we earlier saw space express those American desires that wound their way into the main swelling growth of American life, today we see space take on the flavor of the unconscious self and the desires that self has. Today we see space becoming a spokesman for the other self that formerly stayed inside our sturdy frame of productive life. More, using those unconscious reals of space, that other self is starting to question some of our established ways, especially those having to do with the development of science and technology. Thus the self that existed as human expression and was formerly swallowed into the thickening productive capacity of American life has now established an independent existence and from that vantage point is asking how we might turn our scientific advance into a human form of expression. It is making us question what place we now have for that other self in the whole world of productive dominance.

In this image growing out of our trips to the moon, the human expression of the other self prods the thickening place of science and space.

It's not the first time since we lost our vision of technology as a human force that we are asking about the human values of science. But scraping open some of the raw concerns we have, that question now suggests that our other self provides answers to our problems as well as questions.

In a similar way, many of us are using our other selves to probe the nature of cities. Like Paolo Soleri, some of us are saying that the way for us to turn our unconscious desires into our future is to move flamboyantly into space. We should build right into space, make it serve our needs, make it the agent of our lives in the same way the plains people made their space serve them. In effect, we are suggesting that we make the expression of our other selves become our major form of expression. Soleri's communities start in midair and branch out into units of space we have never before used.

Others still think of our identifiable structures first, as if we can't really ignore our history and all we have inherited. Drawing layers of expression out of those structures, they suggest we widen and deepen our mode of expression by allowing those unexpressed desires to become part of our present. We can live with new modes of expression by extracting unexpressed ones from our locked-in past.

137

If we are to characterize our society today we might well speak of it as filled with resignation and exhilaration, as a society that reveals a burdensome fear of where it is going at the same time it spills off an airy confidence in its new expression. At the very same time we feel sure of ourselves and spinning along on top of the world we also feel how little energy we have and how unable and trapped we may be. We find it easy to scoff at the idea that we could build new systems of life, just as we find it easy to think of a dawning new age. Stretching ourselves between hesitancy and certainty we come up with no answers to our problems at the same time that we provide many. Cynical and beaten on the one hand, we also feel a ferment. It's not as if we live with different trends, which is true of any society, but that our differences take us in divergent directions. We feel two separate tugs on our lives. Emptied of all we could possibly do, we feel all used up at the same time that we generate new forms of expression.

In the years of our counter-culture, roughly from 1920 to 1970, we might have gotten upset if we heard or thought of ourselves as schizoid. After all, if we wanted to be part of the proud norm of American life we couldn't live in two parts, nor could we risk not becoming part of that proud norm. Didn't we even run risk out of our lives as we tried to steady ourselves by countering that swelling mainstream? We couldn't take the chance of breaking ourselves in two, of splitting ourselves up. When we did we considered it abnormal.

But today we all recognize our double-pronged existence and even though one part of us often wants to squelch the images of such existence, or make believe such an existence doesn't exist, we also incorporate that two-headed figure into our great big bag of assumptions and stride forth and call it our movement, thrust, and design.

But if we can really make that other self, that expressive flow of life, become the foundation for a new society, then we will have turned the corner on our used up state of existence. For once we think of transforming our unconscious expressions into ways of determining scientific advance and designing actual communities, then we're really thinking of building a new major stream of life out of all our other selves' germinating expressions. Further, urging new systems of life to grow in the midst of our old, we would be stretching the very dimensions of our society, widening the limits that have always contained our various forms of expression. In addition to freeing us up, our double-pronged life would open the question of just who is free, how free we might be, and how responsible we are to our other selves and the new minor society growing all around us. More than simply expanding our expression, our double-pronged life would enable us to widen our vision of how free we can be.

For the past fifty years we've considered ourselves pretty

decent when we let more people use the freedom we knew. But hanging onto that minimal self-congratulatory expression, we've forfeited our concern with freedom itself. We've even become tangled into arguments of just who is or should be free, staying the growth of freedom as we bargained for new ways to split up our old conception. But if we can let our other self become part of the foundation of our lives, if we can make it stand as a new full-bodied part of our existence and add to our conception of what a person and society is, then we will be on the verge of expanding our conception of freedom for the first time in a century.

List of Illustrations